DINOSAURS
— FROM —
HEAD TO TAIL

...cey Roderick

...anchai Moriya

FRANKLIN WATTS
LONDON•SYDNEY

What dinosaur had
a head like this?

A Parasaurolophus!

With a long, curved crest on its head, the Parasaurolophus (PA-ruh-SAW-ruh-lo-fus) might have been the kind of dinosaur that liked to blow its own trumpet! Some scientists think these dinos communicated by pushing air through the hollow tubes in their crests to make low noises that sounded something like foghorns.

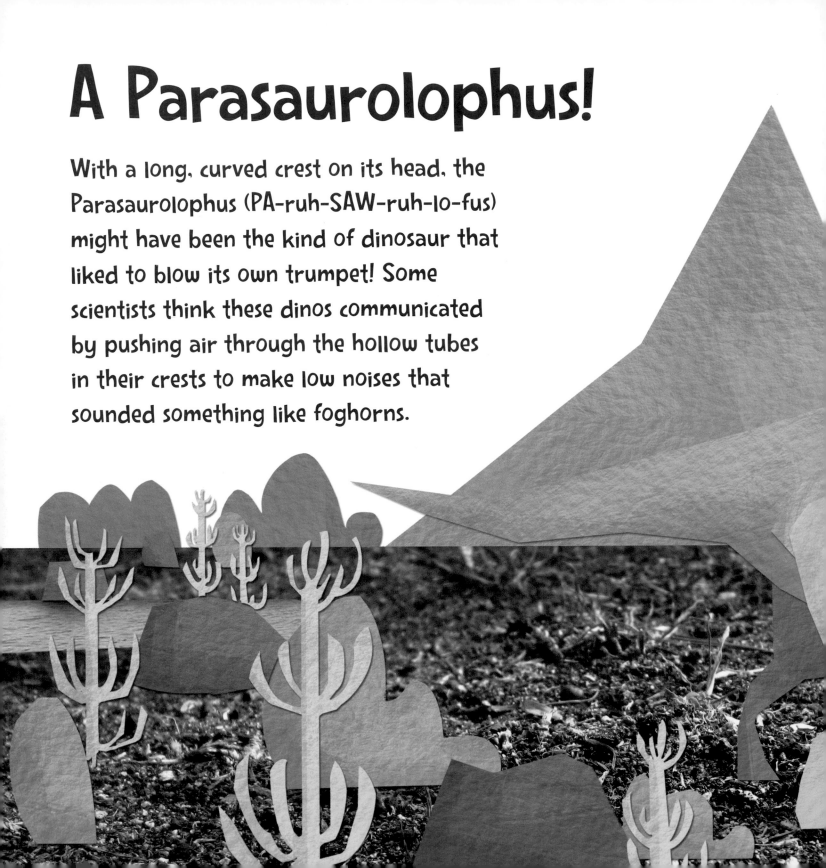

What dinosaur

had jaws like this?

A Tyrannosaurus!

The Tyrannosaurus (ti-ran-uh-SAW-rus) had the most powerful bite of any land animal that has ever lived — up to ten times more powerful than a crocodile's! With a jaw full of 50 to 60 sharp, jagged teeth made for chomping through flesh and bones, it's no surprise that its name means Tyrant Lizard.

What dinosaur had a neck like this?

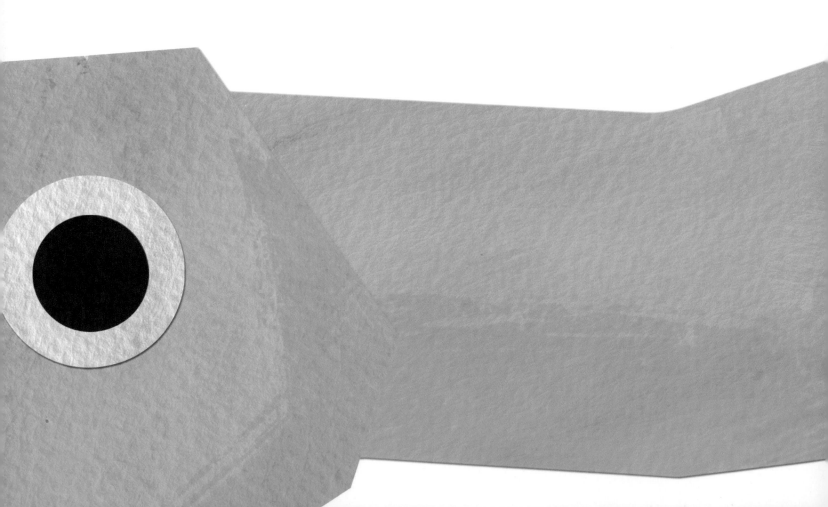

A Diplodocus!

With a neck that stretched about 6 metres, the Diplodocus (dip-lo-DOH-kus) was one of the longest dinosaurs. Such a long neck would have been very difficult to lift up high, so the Diplodocus probably ate plants and trees near the ground. But since it could move its neck from side to side, it covered a big area while standing in just one spot.

What dinosaur had a **back** like this?

A Stegosaurus!

The Stegosaurus (steg-uh-SAW-rus) had two rows of sharp-edged plates running down its back. Scientists think the plates might have been a built-in heating and cooling system. If the dino needed to warm up, the plates soaked up heat from the sun. Or if it needed to cool down, the plates let off extra heat. The rows of plates might also have been a way for the Stegosauruses to recognise each other, as well as scare off any predators thinking about eating them.

What dinosaur had wings like this?

None!

These wings belong to the Pteranodon (teh-RAN-oh-don), which was not actually a dinosaur. But Pteranodons were close relatives of the dinosaurs and lived during the same time period. Pteranodons flew with wings made of thin skin that stretched from their long fourth fingers to the tops of their legs.

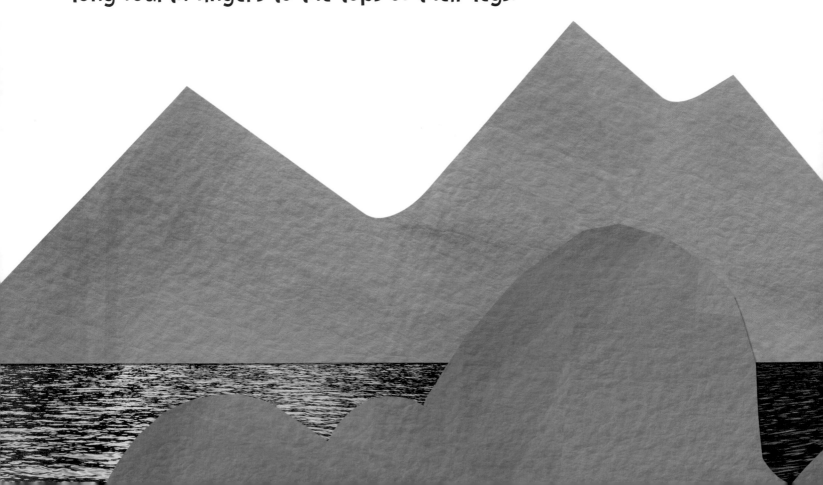

What dinosaur had claws like this?

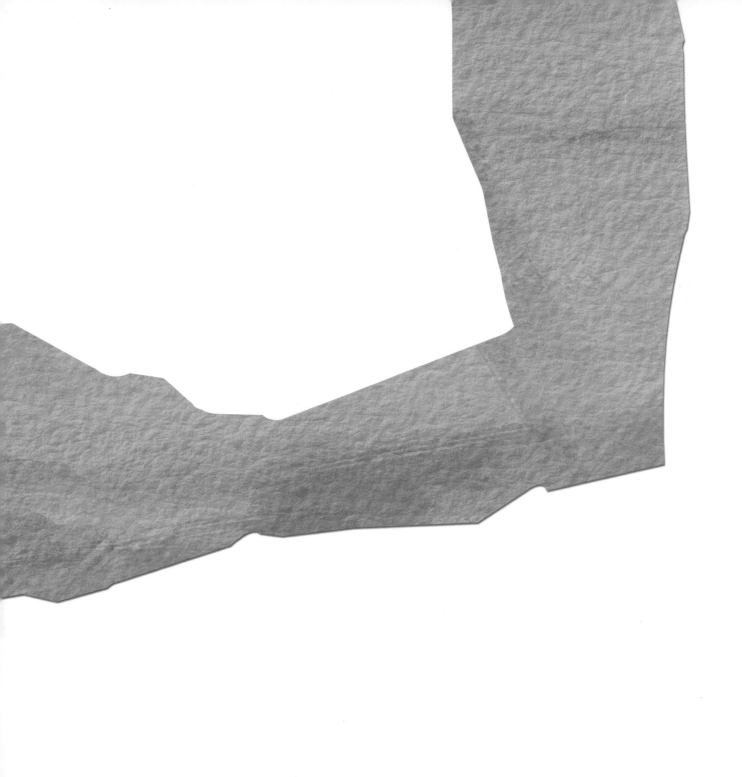

A Therizinosaurus!

The Therizinosaurus (THER-uh-ZEEN-uh-SAW-rus) had three giant claws on each of its front feet. The claws may have measured up to 1 metre — about as long as a cricket bat. No wonder this plant-eater's claws are thought to be the longest of any animal that has ever lived!

What dinosaur had legs like this?

A Giganotosaurus!

The Giganotosaurus (jig-a-NOT-uh-SAW-rus) used its powerful, muscular legs to chase its prey. This massive meat-eater was what scientists call a biped, an animal that gets around using two legs. It was even bigger than another famous meat-eating biped — the Tyrannosaurus.

What dinosaur
had a tail like this?

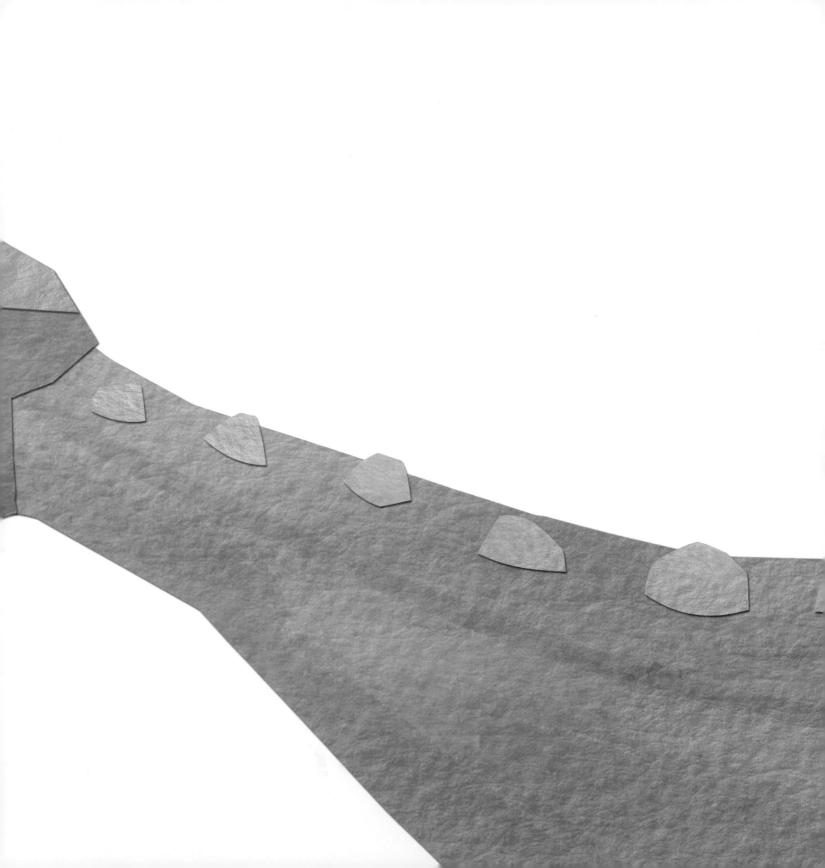

An Ankylosaurus!

The Ankylosaurus (ang-KI-low-SAW-rus) probably used the rounded, bony ball on the end of its tail to protect itself from attacking predators. Scientists think that by swinging its tail from side to side like a club, it could have actually broken the bones of another dinosaur.

Other Awesome Dinosaurs

The Triceratops (tri-SARE-uh-tops) had three horns and a bony frill on its huge head.

The plant-eating Corythosaurus (caw-rith-oh-SAW-rus) had a beak-like mouth filled with hundreds of teeth for chewing.

Bony armour covered the Edmontonia (ED-mon-TONE-ee-ah), including large, ridged plates that protected its neck.

Meat-eating Spinosaurus (SPINE-oh-SAW-rus) had a tall, spiny sail running down its back.

The Iguanodon (ig-WHA-noh-don) had a cone-shaped thumb spike on each hand.

The chicken-sized Compsognathus (komp-sog-NA-thus) ran around on two skinny legs.

Like many large dinosaurs that walked on two feet, the Allosaurus (al-oh-SAW-rus) had a thick, heavy tail that helped with balance.

For my Owenosaurus (OH-wen-oh-SORE-us) — S.R.

For Mommy and Papa — K.M.

Acknowledgments
Many thanks to David C. Evans, Ph.D., Curator of Vertebrate
Palaeontology, Department of Natural History (Palaeobiology), Royal
Ontario Museum, and to Donald Henderson, Ph.D., Curator
of Dinosaurs, Royal Tyrrell Museum, for generously sharing
their time and expertise to review this manuscript.

This edition published
by Franklin Watts
338 Euston Road
London NW1 3BH

Franklin Watts Australia
Level 17/207 Kent Street
Sydney, NSW 2000

Text © 2015 Kids Can Press
Illustrations © 2015 Kwanchai Moriya

Published by permission of Kids Can Press Ltd.
Toronto, Canada.

Edited by Stacey Roderick
Designed by Julia Naimska

A CIP catalogue record for this book
is available from the British Library.

ISBN 978 1 4451 4242 5

Manufactured in Shenzhen, China, in 11/2014 by Imago

Franklin Watts is a division of
Hachette Children's Books,
an Hachette UK company.
www.hachette.co.uk